Other Books by Louis Simpson

The
BEST HOUR
of the
NIGHT

POEMS

Louis Simpson

Ticknor & Fields

NEW HAVEN AND NEW YORK

1983

Library of Congress Cataloging in Publication Data

Simpson, Louis Aston Marantz, 1923-
The best hour of the night.

I. Title.
PS3537.I75B4   1983   811'.54   83-5075
ISBN 0-89919-203-3
ISBN 0-89919-204-1 (pbk.)

Printed in the United States of America

V 10 9 8 7 6 5 4 3 2 1

The author thanks the editors of the following publications
for granting permission to reprint.

Crazy Horse: "Akhmatova's Husband." *Cumberland Poetry
Review:* "Damned Suitcase." *The Georgia Review:* "A Fine
Day for Straw Hats." *The Hampden-Sydney Poetry Review:*
"Bernie." *Harvard Magazine:* "Ed." *The Hudson Review:*
"Physical Universe," "How to Live on Long Island," "The
Previous Tenant," "In a Time of Peace." *The Iowa Review:*
"Quiet Desperation." *New Letters:* "The Eleventh Com-
mandment." *Northern Lights:* "The Unwritten Poem." *The
Ohio Review:* "Encounter on the 7:07." *Pequod:* "Red-
avoiding Pictures," "In Otto's Basement." *Ploughshares:* "The
Champion Single Sculls," "The Gardener." *Poetry East:* "A
Remembrance of Things Past." *The Virginia Quarterly Re-
view:* "Periodontics," "Elegy for Jake." *Zephyr:* "Reflections
in a Spa."

For Susan with love

CONTENTS

I
PHYSICAL
UNIVERSE

PHYSICAL UNIVERSE

He woke at five and, unable
to go back to sleep,
went downstairs.

A book was lying on the table
where his son had done his homework.
He took it into the kitchen,
made coffee, poured himself a cup,
and settled down to read.

"There was a local eddy in the swirling gas
of the primordial galaxy,
and a cloud was formed, the protosun,
as wide as the present solar system.

This contracted. Some of the gas
formed a diffuse, spherical nebula,
a thin disk, that cooled and flattened.
Pulled one way by its own gravity,
the other way by the sun,
it broke, forming smaller clouds,
the protoplanets. Earth
was 2,000 times as wide as it is now."

*The earth was without form, and void,
and darkness was upon the face of the deep.*

*

"Then the sun began to shine,
dispelling the gases and vapors,
shrinking the planets, melting earth,
separating iron and silicate
to form the core and mantle.
Continents appeared . . ."

history, civilization,
the discovery of America
and the settling of Green Harbor,
bringing us to Tuesday, the seventh of July.

Tuesday, the day they pick up the garbage!
He leapt into action,
took the garbage bag out of its container,
tied it with a twist of wire,
and carried it out to the toolshed,
taking care not to let the screen door slam,
and put it in the large garbage can
that was three-quarters full.
He kept it in the toolshed so the raccoons
couldn't get at it.

He carried the can out to the road,
then went back into the house
and walked around, picking up newspapers
and fliers for: "Thompson Seedless Grapes,
California's finest sweet eating";

"Scott Bathroom Tissue";

"Legislative report from Senator Ken LaValle."

He put all this paper in a box,
and emptied the waste baskets in the two
downstairs bathrooms,
and the basket in the study.

He carried the box out to the road,
taking care not to let the screen door slam,
and placed the box next to the garbage.

Now let the garbage men come!

*

4

He went back upstairs.
Susan said, "Did you put out the garbage?"
But her eyes were closed.
She was sleeping, yet could speak in her sleep,
ask a question, even answer one.

"Yes," he said, and climbed into bed.
She turned around to face him,
with her eyes still closed.

He thought, perhaps she's an oracle,
speaking from the Collective Unconscious.
He said to her, "Do you agree with Darwin
that people and monkeys have a common ancestor?
Or should we stick to the Bible?"

She said, "Did you take out the garbage?"

"Yes," he said, for the second time.
Then thought about it. Her answer
had something in it of the sublime.
Like a *koan* . . . the kind of irrelevance
a Zen master says to the disciple
who is asking riddles of the universe.

He put his arm around her,
and she continued to breathe evenly
from the depths of sleep.

HOW TO LIVE ON LONG ISLAND

Lilco, $75.17;
Mastercard, $157.89;
Sunmark Industries, $94.03 . . .

Jim is paying his bills.
He writes out a check
and edges it into the envelope
provided by the company.
They always make them too small.

The print in the little box
in the top right corner informs him:
"The Post Office will not deliver
mail without proper postage."
They seem to know that the public
is composed of thieves and half-wits.

He seals the last envelope,
licks a stamp, sticks it on,
and with a feeling of virtue,
a necessary task accomplished,
takes the checks out to the mailbox.

It's a cool, clear night in Fall,
lights flickering through the leaves.
He thinks, all these families
with their situation comedies:
husbands writing checks,
wives studying fund-raising,
children locked in their rooms
listening to the music that appeals to them,
remind me of . . . fireflies
that shine for a night and die.

Of all these similar houses
what shall be left? Not even stones.

One could almost understand the pharaohs
with their pyramids and obelisks.

Every month when he pays his bills
Jim Bandy becomes a philosopher.
The rest of the time he's OK.

Jim has a hobby: fishing.
Last year he flew to Alaska.
Cold the salmon stream,
dark the Douglas firs,
and the pure stars are cold.

A bear came out of the forest.
Jim had two salmon . . . he threw one
but the bear kept coming.
He threw the other . . . it stopped.

The fish that are most memorable
he mounts, with a brass plate
giving the name and place and date:
Chinook Salmon, Red Salmon,
Brown Trout, Grouper,
Barracuda, Hammerhead Shark.

They do a lot of drinking in Alaska.
He saw thirty or forty lying drunk
in the street. And on the plane . . .

They cannot stand living in Alaska,
and he cannot stand Long Island
without flying to Alaska.

ENCOUNTER ON THE 7:07

He got on at Cold Spring Harbor
and took the seat next to mine —
a man of about forty, with a suntan.

The doctor said, "You need a vacation."
His wife said, "It's an opportunity,
we can visit my sister in Florida."

He played golf every day
and they visited the Everglades.
Trees standing out of the swamp
with moss and vines hanging down,
ripples moving through the water . . .

An alligator is different from a crocodile,
it has a broad head, et cetera.

*

There's a car card advertising
"Virginia Slims" — a photographer's model
got up to look like a cowgirl
in boots and a ten-gallon hat.
She's kneeling with a cigarette in her hand
and a smile — in spite of the warning
printed below: "The Surgeon General
has determined that cigarette smoking
is dangerous to your health."

It's the American way
not to be daunted — to smoke cigarettes
and rope cattle all you want.

The man sitting next to me,
whose name is Jerry — Jerry DiBello —

8

observes that he doesn't smoke cigarettes,
he smokes cigars. "Look at Winston Churchill.
He smoked cigars every day of his life,
and he lived to be over eighty."

*

Wordsworth said that the passions
of people who live in the country
are incorporated with the beautiful
and permanent forms of nature.
In the suburbs they are incorporated
with the things you see from the train:
rows of windshields . . . a factory . . .
a housing development, all the houses
alike, either oblong or square,
like the houses and hotels in a game of *Monopoly*.

A crane, bright orange, bearing the name "Slattery" . . .

"Feldman," a sign says, "Lumber."
A few miles further on . . .
"Feldman, Wood Products."

*

"The Old Coachman Bar and Grill" . . .

His family used to own a restaurant
on 25A . . . DiBello's.

His father came from Genoa
as a seaman, and jumped ship.
In the middle of the night
he went up on deck,
put his shoes and clothes in a bag,
hung it around his neck,
stood on the rail, and jumped.

9

He swam to shore and hid in the bushes.
The next day he started walking . . .
came to a restaurant and asked for a job
washing dishes. Ten years later
he owned the restaurant.

Jerry didn't go into the business.
He sells automobiles,
has his own Buick-Pontiac showroom.
It's hard to make a living these days.
The government ought to clamp down on the Japanese
flooding the market with their Datsuns.

But I'm not listening — I'm on deck,
looking at the lights of the harbor.
A sea wind fans my cheek.
I hear the waves chuckling
against the side of the ship.

I grasp the iron stanchion,
climb onto the rail,
take a deep breath,
and jump.

*

I've brought along *Ulysses*
and am just passing the time of day
with old Troy of the D.M.P.
when be damned but a bloody sweep comes along
and near drives his gear in my eye.

"An *olla putrida* . . .
old fags and cabbage-stumps of quotations,"
said Lawrence. Drawing a circle about himself
and Frieda . . . building an ark,
envisioning the Flood.

But the Flood may be long coming.
In the meantime there is life
every day, and Ennui.

Ever since the middle class
and money have ruled our world
we have been desolate.

                              Like Emma Bovary
in the beech-copse, watching her dog
yapping about, chasing a butterfly.

A feeling of being alone
and separate from the world . . .
"alienation" psychiatrists call it.
Religion would say, this turning away
from life is the life of the soul.

This is why Joyce is such a great writer:
he shows a life of fried bread
and dripping "like a boghole,"
and art that rises out of life
and flies toward the sun,

transfiguring as it flies
the reality . . . Joe Hynes,
Alf Bergan, Bob Doran,
and the saint of the quotidian
himself, Leopold Bloom.

                              *

Jerry has a gang who meet every Saturday
to play poker. For friendly stakes . . .
you can lose twenty or thirty dollars,
that's all. It's the camaraderie
that counts.

They talk about the ball game,
politics, tell the latest jokes . . .

One of the guys sells insurance,
another works at the firehouse.

As if reading my mind . . .
"Don't take us for a bunch of bobos."
There's a chemist who works for Westinghouse,
and a lawyer who's on permanent retainer
with the Long Island Lighting Company.

What, he asks, do I do?

I tell him, and he says, it figures.
The way I was so lost in a book
he could see that I live in a different world.

*

In Florida after the storm
the whole area for miles inland
was littered with trees and telephone poles,
wrecked automobiles, houses that had blown down.
There was furniture, chairs and sofas,
lying in the street, buried in mud.

For days afterwards they were still finding bodies.

When he went for a walk
the shore looked as though it had been swept
with a broom. The sky was clear,
the sun was shining, and the sea was calm.

He felt that he was alone with the universe.
He, Jerry DiBello, was at one with God.

DAMNED SUITCASE

Her suitcase wasn't in the car,
it was back at the house.
"Everyone," he told her, "above the age of twelve

takes care of her own suitcase.
I can't do everything for you."
She said, "You were loading the car,"

and proceeded to show that Milton
was right: *left to herself, if evil thence ensue,
Shee first his weak indulgence will accuse.*

                        *

He had already paid for the boat
and a can of worms.
She sat in the stern, he rowed.

"No," he said, "it's impossible.
We have to go back and get your damned suitcase."
"No," she said, "I'll go back. You go on by yourself."

*Thus they in mutual accusation spent
The fruitless hours, but neither self-condemning,
And of thir vain contést appear'd no end.*

                        *

Who would be so foolish as to argue
that his marriage was ordained?
It was an accident, like everything else.

The one he could have truly loved
may have been living in the next street,
but things were arranged so they would never meet.

13

All our lives depend on some object
that has been misplaced: a handkerchief,
a letter, a goddamned suitcase.

*

At this point it began to rain.
The lake seethed, the shore was invisible,
they huddled in their raincoats.

It stopped, and the sun shone.
They had drifted close to a rock
covered with purple rhododendrons.

The water next to the boat was clear.
You could see to the bottom,
trout, a foot long, gliding between the reeds.

*

He said, "We'll go back to the house,
and start again. We've lost a day . . .
I don't suppose it makes so much difference."

QUIET DESPERATION

At the post office he sees Joe McInnes.
Joe says, "We're having some people over.
It'll be informal. Come as you are."

She is in the middle
of preparing dinner. Tonight
she is trying an experiment:
Hal Burgonyaual — Fish–Potato Casserole.
She has cooked and drained the potatoes
and cut the fish in pieces.
Now she has to "mash potatoes,
add butter and hot milk," et cetera.

He relays Joe's invitation.
"No," she says, "not on your life.
Muriel McInnes is no friend of mine."

It appears that she told Muriel
that the Goldins live above their means,
and Muriel told Mary Goldin.

He listens carefully, to get things right.
The feud between the Andersons and the Kellys
began with Ruth Anderson calling Mike Kelly
a reckless driver. Finally
the Andersons had to sell their house and move.

Social life is no joke.
It can be the only life there is.

*

In the living room the battle of Iwo Jima
is in progress, watched by his son.
Men are dying on the beach,
pinned down by a machine gun.

The marine carrying the satchel charge
falls. Then Sergeant Stryker
picks up the charge and starts running.

Now you are with the enemy machine gun
firing out of the pillbox
as Stryker comes running,
bullets at his heels kicking up dust.
He makes it to the base of the pillbox,
lights the charge, raises up,
and heaves it through the opening.
The pillbox explodes . . .
the NCO's wave, "Move out!"

And he rises to his feet.
He's seen the movie. Stryker gets killed
just as they're raising the flag.

*

A feeling of pressure . . .
There is something that needs to be done
immediately.

        But there is nothing,
only himself. His life is passing,
and afterwards there will be eternity,
silence, and infinite space.

He thinks, "Firewood!" —
and goes to the basement,
takes the Swede-saw off the wall,
and goes outside, to the woodpile.

He carries an armful to the sawhorse
and saws the logs into smaller pieces.
In twenty minutes he has a pile of firewood
cut just the right length.
He carries the cut logs into the house

and arranges them in a neat pile
next to the fireplace.

Then looks around for something else to do,
to relieve the feeling of pressure.

The dog!
He will take the dog for a walk.

*

They make a futile procession . . .
he commanding her to "Heel!" —
she dragging back or straining ahead.

The leaves are turning yellow.
Between the trunks of the trees
the cove is blue, with ripples.
The swans — this year there are seven —
are sailing line astern.

But when you come closer
the rocks above the shore are littered
with daggers of broken glass
where the boys sat on summer nights
and broke beer bottles afterwards.

And the beach is littered, with cans,
containers, heaps of garbage,
newspaper wadded against the sea-wall.
Someone has even dumped a mattress . . .
a definite success!
Some daring guy, some Stryker
in the pickup speeding away.

He cannot bear the sun
going over and going down . . .
the trees and houses vanishing
in quiet every day.

II

The
PREVIOUS
TENANT

THE PREVIOUS TENANT

All that winter it snowed.
The sides of roads were heaped with it.
The nights were quiet. If you stepped outside,
above the dark woods and fields
hung glittering stars and constellations.

My landlord, Stanley, came by now and then
to see how things were going.
I reminded him that the previous tenant
had left boxes full of clothes,
a pair of skis, a rifle,
three shelves of books, and a fishing pole.

All right, he said, he'd get in touch with him.

I said, he must have left in a hurry.

A hurry? Stanley considered.
His eyes gleamed under bushy eyebrows.
Satanic. But I happened to know that Stanley
wouldn't hurt a fly. All that Fall
I'd seen him trying to think of something
to persuade some raccoons to quit the premises —
everything short of a gun.

"McNeil was a bit disorganized,"
he said with a smile.

I asked if he'd like some coffee,
and he said yes. While I was making it
he talked about the previous tenant.

2

A doctor named Hugh McNeil
came on the staff at Mercy Hospital
and bought a house in Point Mercy.

Hugh and Nancy fitted right in . . .
people liked them.
Helen Knox, whose husband was vice-president
of the National Maritime Bank,
called on Nancy and invited her
to join the Garden Club.
Then they were asked to join the Golf Club.
(The Levines, on the other hand, hadn't been invited.
After two years of Point Mercy
they sold their house and moved back to Queens.)

The McNeils had children: Tom, fourteen,
and Laurie, nine and a half, nearly ten.
McNeil was one of the fathers on Saturday
dashing about. He drove a green Land Rover
as though he were always on safari
with the children and an Irish setter.

Nancy was nice . . . blonde,
and intelligent — she'd been to Wellesley.
She took on the job of secretary
of the Garden Club, that nobody wanted,
and helped organize the dance at the Yacht Club
on July the Fourth, for Hugh had joined that too.
He bought a "Cal" Thirty Martini–rigged sloop,
and with Tom as crew went sailing.
They came in fifth in the Martha Woodbury
Perpetual Trophy.

        Nancy didn't sail,
it made her seasick. She sat on the patio
with her knitting till the boats hove in sight,
then went down to the basin.

McNeil spoke at village meetings
with moderation and common sense.
Once he argued for retaining
the Latin teacher at the high school.
Latin, he explained, was still useful
for medicine and law, and a foundation
for good English. They heard him out
and voted to let the Latin teacher go
and remodel the gymnasium.
McNeil accepted defeat gracefully.
That was one of the things they liked about him.

The residents of Point Mercy
are proud of their village
with its beautiful homes and gardens
and bird sanctuary.
Contrary to what people say
about the suburbs, they appreciate culture.
Hugh McNeil was an example . . .
doing the shopping, going to the club,
a man in no way different from themselves,
husband and family man
and good neighbor, who nevertheless spoke Latin.

3

Her name was Irene Davis.
Before she married it was Cristiano.
"I met her once," said Helen Knox.
"Harry introduced her to me
at the bank. A dark woman . . .
I think, a touch of the tar brush."

There is no accounting for tastes
observed Sandie Bishop.

The woman's husband was an invalid
and patient of Dr. McNeil.

The green Land Rover had been seen
parked outside the Davises' house
in the afternoon, in the evening,
and once — this was hilarious — the doctor
ran out of gas in that part of town
at three in the morning. He didn't have cash
or credit cards on him, and had to walk
to the nearest open service station.
The attendant let him have a gallon.
"I've been in the same fix," he told McNeil,
"you can pay me some other time."

The attendant talked, and the story
got back to Point Mercy.
"It's a scandal," said Sandie.
"Do you think Nancy knows?"

Helen said, "I'm sure she does."

"Someone should have a talk with him,"
Sandie said. She remembered
with some excitement, the occasion
when a resident of Point Mercy
had been thinking of selling his house
to a family that was black.
Every morning he would find garbage
dumped on his lawn. The prospective buyer
received an anonymous letter,
and that was the end of that.

"Let's not be hasty," said Helen
who was president of the Garden Club
and had more experience.
"These things have a way of working themselves out."

4

One day there was a sensation:
Dr. McNeil had been mugged,
beaten and left by the road.

"Mugged?" said the service station attendant.
This was long after the event.

He looked around, but there was no one
in hearing distance, only the dog,
a hound that wandered around
with an infected ear, snapping at flies.
All at once it perked up its ears
and went running. It must have smelled something
mixed with the odor of gasoline
and dust . . . a delirious
fragrance of sensual life.

The attendant leaned closer
and said in a conspiratorial voice,
"He was never mugged.
It was Irene Davis's brothers,
the Cristianos. They had him beat up."

He knew about gangsters. They would beat up a guy
to warn him. The next time it was curtains.

5

So McNeil was in the hospital
with two broken ribs, black eyes,
and a missing tooth.

At the next meeting of the Garden Club
the president said she was as broad-minded
as anyone, but this . . .

here she paused as though it were beneath her
to find words for such low behavior . . .
had brought violence into their midst.

Sandie moved they send a delegation
to the hospital, to demand McNeil's
immediate resignation.

The next day four of the members
called on Dr. Abrahams, chief of staff,
and told him what they wanted.
A short man, with hair on his face,
all the time they were talking he kept turning
from one to the other, and grinning,
like some sort of monkey, Sandie said afterwards.

He thanked them for their concern.
But McNeil's private life —
not that he knew anything about it —
had nothing to do with his work
or his position here at the hospital.
If they would take his advice
they would be careful what they said —
they might find themselves charged
with libel. Speaking, he was sure,
for the entire staff, they were fortunate
to have a surgeon of Hugh McNeil's caliber.

Could he be of service in anything else?
No? Then would they please excuse him . . .
it looked like a busy day.

They were halfway to the parking lot.
"What can you expect?" said Helen.
"It was bad enough letting them in,
but to make one chief of staff!"

She knew how to put what they were feeling
into words. This was why

she was president — elected not once
or twice . . . this was her third term in office.

6

Then Nancy sued for divorce.
She had all the evidence she needed:
her husband had been with Irene Davis
in Providence, Rhode Island,
when he was supposed to be in Boston
attending a medical conference.

This was when he moved into the cottage.
It consisted of a small bedroom,
living room, bathroom, kitchen.
Thoreau, who recommends sleeping in the box
railroad workers keep their tools in,
would have found this house commodious.

I could imagine him coming home . . .
putting some fries on a metal sheet
and sliding it into the oven
set at 350 degrees.
Sprinkling a couple of chops
with pepper and garlic.
Deciding which frozen vegetable . . .
say, spinach. Putting the block
in a saucer with water and salt.
Making a salad . . . but this would mean
slicing tomatoes, radishes, scallions,
and washing lettuce. There would be times
when he just couldn't be bothered.

He would have a drink, then a second.
You have to be careful not to make it three
and four. On the other hand
you shouldn't be too careful,
or like Robinson Crusoe you may find yourself

taking pride in the neatness and efficiency
of your domestic arrangements:
all your bowls made out of gourds
lined up on a shelf according to size.
Ditto your spoons.
"A place for everything," you say to the parrot,
"and everything in its place."

Bake the French fries,
boil the frozen vegetable, broil the lamb chops.
You can prepare a nourishing dinner
in twenty minutes, and eat it in five
while reading the *Times* or watching *Charlie's Angels*.

He would watch TV again after dinner.
My God, he'd say to the walls,
it can't be this bad. But it was.
He'd turn it off and pick up a book.
Now that he had plenty of time
he could catch up on the ones he'd missed
when they came out: titles like *Future Shock*
and *The Greening of America*.

Then he was on an express train
racing to the end of the line,
a flash and a moment of excruciating
pain. He was paralyzed,
helpless to move a leg or an arm.

And woke, having fallen asleep
in his chair, to hear the dripping
of snow melting on the roof.

On nights when he couldn't sleep
he'd watch the late late show.
In the dark night of the soul,
says F. Scott Fitzgerald,
it is always three in the morning.
Hemingway says, it isn't so bad . . .

in fact, the best hour of the night
once you've reconciled yourself to insomnia
and stopped worrying about your sins.
And I say that insomnia can be
a positive joy if you're tuned in to *Dames*
or *Gold Diggers of 1933.*
I remember seeing *The Producers*
at three in the morning, and practically
falling out of bed. There are pleasures
known to none but late late movie-goers,
moments of the purest absurdity,
such as, in an otherwise boring movie
starring the Marx Brothers, the "Tenement Symphony"
as sung by Tony Martin.

So there he was, watching Busby Berkeley's
electrically lighted waterfalls,
and the Warner Brothers cuties
viewed from underneath, treading water.

"Ain't we got fun!" shrieked the parrot,
and the goat gave a great bound.

7

Behind the Perry Masons and Agatha Christies
I came across a packet of letters.
It was like being a detective.

When Irene's husband came home
from the hospital, he was confined
to his bed, by doctor's orders.
And McNeil was the doctor.
"Call me at home," said Irene.
"There is no problem about telephone calls."

I copied some of the passages.
They might come in useful. There was an idea for a novel

I'd had for years: A *Bovary of the Sierras* . . .
The Bovary of Evanston . . . *The Bovary of Green Harbor.*

There was a paragraph about some flowers
and his cock that might have been conceived
by the author of *Lady Chatterley's Lover.*
It went to show that when an idea
has genuine merit, individuals
far removed in space and time
come upon it independently.

She even knew her Bible:
"When my beloved slipped his hand through the latch-hole
my bowels stirred within me."

Rumor was right. It was her brothers
who had McNeil beaten up.
She told him that he wasn't to see her
ever again. She feared for his life.
"Irene . . . signing off."

But she didn't sign off. Here she was again.
"If you have a new woman in your life
or you've gone back to your wife
I don't want to muck things up.
This is just a peacepipe, kid —
send me a smoke signal
if I'm getting in the way of anything.
Cheerio, Irene."

Then they picked up again where they'd left off.
They had been with each other
yesterday. She could still feel him inside her.

I was beginning to be afraid
for him. For her. For both of them.

8

Stanley telephoned to say that McNeil
was coming to pick up his things.

I put the books in cartons,
and piled the cartons and the rest of his things
next to the door: the boxes of clothes,
the skis, the fishing pole,
and the rifle — I was loath to part with it,
the way America was greening.

The next day my predecessor
arrived. A man of forty
with red hair . . . looking slightly angry.
Suspicious. I couldn't put my finger on it.

He was accompanied by a young woman
wearing jeans and a sweater.
She was fair, and had a friendly smile.
"It was good of you to take care
of Hugh's things," she said. "Wasn't it, Hugh?"
"O yes," he said. "Thanks."

I helped them carry things out
to the station wagon. It was snowing again . . .
not flakes, but particles, coming down fast
at an angle, like rain or hail.

They drove away.
She waved. He looked straight ahead.
It appeared he was back on the track
once more, after his derailment.
With a woman of the right kind at his side
to give him a nudge. "Say thanks!"

9

It is always that famous day and year
at the Colony Inn . . . a brick fireplace,
rough-hewn beams, and pewter candlesticks.
From the ceiling hang the flags
of the thirteen original colonies.

The waitresses wear bonnets and muslin gowns
that hang straight from the shoulder
to the floor, leaving their arms and elbows
exposed. Some of the older waitresses
seem to resent being made to dress
like children. Their movements are slow.

One of them arrived finally
to take our order and departed,
moving with slow steps
as befitted an early American.

Maggie said, "Don't look now!
By the window . . . that's Irene Davis,
the woman McNeil had the affair with."

I looked around the room casually
and let my gaze come to rest
on Irene.

They said she was dark. What they hadn't said
was that the darkness, jet-black hair,
was set off by a skin like snow,
like moonlight in a dark field glimmering.
Her features were . . . fine. She wouldn't have been
out of place in an Italian villa
with walls five feet thick, and chickens
roosting on the furniture . . . the family
crowded into three rooms upstairs . . .

a *contessa,* married to the invalid son
of impoverished aristocracy.

I wondered what she would have thought
if she'd known I'd read her letters.

There were two people with her:
an old woman with white hair
who looked as though she'd just got off
the boat from Palermo . . .
and a man, he must be Irene's brother . . .
the same black hair and white complexion.
But what in her looked romantic,
in him spelled murder. He was thin
and sinewy . . . wearing a green jacket,
dark green shirt, white tie.

I imagined he was being tolerant
of the restaurant . . . these assholes
with their consommés and casseroles,
their salads consisting of lettuce
and cottage cheese . . . And what was this
for chrissake? Sweet potato
with marshmallow on top . . . you call this food?

But he was on his best behavior.
He didn't pull an automatic
and blow holes through the flags
of the thirteen original colonies.

Irene must have felt me staring.
She turned . . . her eyes met mine
for a few seconds. I had an impression
of . . . defiance. "What do you want?"

I quickly looked away.

10

Maggie was meeting a friend
at three. It was now two-thirty.

So we walked around Island Bay.
The village has been reconstructed
to preserve a Colonial atmosphere.
At the crest of a slope facing the bay
stands the post office. This at least
is authentic. It has four columns,
white of course, and a big golden eagle
above the entrance. On either side
in a crescent, there are shops
with signs lettered in gold:
Optometrist, Pharmacy, Antiques . . .
There's a shop selling Irish linen
and wool. Another selling jewelry
and notions . . . Royal Doulton . . .
little statues of Colonial women
in hoopskirts and wigs,
and the figure of a young girl
in shorts, taking a swing at a golf ball.

The slope goes down to a road.
Between this and the bay
stands a gazebo, an open dome
housing a bust of Hercules.
This, they say, was a ship's figurehead.
All but the bearded head
is a reconstruction . . . some local artist
has added a muscular torso
and draped over one shoulder
the skin of the Nemean lion.
A sillier, more pathetic monster
it would be hard to imagine,
with his doggy nose and wide-open eyes
that seem to say, Look at me.
I never did any harm.

This monument to our culture,
believe it or not, had been vandalized . . .
battered and gashed.
Whoever did it must have used a hammer
or an axe.

I said, "Boys will be boys."

"I'm sure," Maggie said, "it wasn't anyone
from around here."

I wasn't so sure. Our high schools
every year turn out their quota of vandals
and thieves. Not to mention illiterates.
You don't have to go into New York City . . .

How, she said, could I be so cynical?

I said, why was it
that when you told the truth
people accused you of being cynical?

We were on our way to having a quarrel.
I didn't want to. I liked Maggie,
with her quizzical way of looking at me,
her air of calm, unclouded judgment,
her mouth that turned down at one corner
when she smiled.

But now she wasn't smiling.
She said, "It's your attitude.
Like what you said in the restaurant
about Hugh McNeil and the Davis woman
being better than the rest of us."

She had her back to the post office.
The wings of the golden eagle
seemed to spring out of her shoulders.
I was filled with a sense of the ridiculous.

She sensed it, and became really angry.
"I know, you prefer vulgar people.
Anyone who tries to be decent and respectable
is either a hypocrite or a fool."

So we had our quarrel.
Then a car drove up and stopped.
It was Helen Knox. She leaned over
and opened the door for Maggie.

"Good afternoon," she said to me,
very cool. I knew what she thought of me
and my writing. A friend told me —
for writers have such friends.

She said, "I thought I ought to read
one of his novels. But I couldn't bring myself
to finish it. Why write about
such ordinary things?

What with chauffeuring the children
and entertaining Harry's friends,
if I find time to read, it has to be something
that takes me out of myself.

You have to be selective —
this is why I read the *New Yorker*, and *Time*,
and subscribe to the Book of the Month."

III
The
BEST HOUR
of the
NIGHT

THE ELEVENTH COMMANDMENT

"Do you know the eleventh commandment?"
Harry asks. I shake my head.
I'm the straight man in these encounters.

"The eleventh commandment,"
he says, "is, 'Don't get caught.' "

Then, as I recall, everyone laughs.

*

He hands a hundred-dollar bill
to his older boy, to buy fireworks
from a man from New Jersey
who's selling them out of his truck.

Then he and I and the boys
are setting them off. Rockets
go climbing with a whoosh
and bang! The sky above Green Harbor
is lit red, white, and blue.
Bright flares come glimmering down.
People have come out of their houses
and stand in the street, looking up.

A thoroughly illegal operation
that everyone is taking part in . . .
What could be more appropriate
on the Fourth of July? More American?

*

If you want to accomplish anything
in this world, you can't be too particular.

Ethics are nice to have on a wall, in Latin,
but Latin won't meet a payroll.

39

And don't give me any of that
about the system. It's the same in Russia.

*

When the financial scandal burst
in the light of the flash he was still smiling,
"confident that he and his partners
would be cleared of all violations" —

kickbacks, misapplication of funds,
conspiracy, fraud, concealment, wire fraud,
falsified books and records, and
interstate transportation of stolen property.

*

"I miss him," she says.

"What makes me sick
is the way everyone's turned against him.

Let me tell you about the people
next door. They're stealing bricks
from a building site. Every night
they drive over and steal some more.
They're making a patio and an outdoor barbecue."

Her younger boy, Kyle, comes over
and stands watchfully in front of me.
He is wearing a spaceman's helmet
and carrying a ray gun or laser.

"Hi there," I say to him.
What else do you say to a six-year-old?

PERIODONTICS

"Am I hurting you?" says Eubie.
I shake my head, no,
for I've learned not to show pain.
At the school of dental hygiene
where Eubie got her diploma
they teach them not to be put off
by a wince or gathering tear
but to stay on the sensitive spot
and . . . "Festina lente" . . . be thorough.

I try to think of something else . . .
"P.C.," the initials
on the dental unit in front of me.

These were Paula's initials.
The Chapmans lived on Riverside Drive
obliquely across from the sign
for Spry. "Spry for Baking"
it said, and blinked off,
then on again. "For Frying."

The apartment had wall-to-wall carpeting
and dark brown furniture waxed so it shone.
There was a cabinet with glass doors
full of objets d'art: an elephant
carved out of ivory, a wooden Russian doll.
There was an old windup Victrola
with hits from Broadway musicals
and "classics," Gershwin and Tchaikovsky.
A bookcase held *The Wandering Jew* by Eugène Sue.

Mr. Chapman had studied for the Ph.D.
but universities wouldn't hire a Jew
so instead he went into business.

"How are we doing?" says Eubie.
OK, I nod, fine.
I call her my Buchenwald Baby . . .
with her eyes of cornflower blue
that never look into mine
directly, but at some view
slightly to the right or to the left
as she travels with the cavitron.

*

"Oh my God," said Paula,
"he isn't even wearing a tie!"

She looked like a fairy princess
in a bright blue gown
that showed that her breasts
had budded, as Proust would say.

I was wearing a suit
but it was brown and tired.
And I had no tie . . .
I hadn't thought it was required.

"He can wear one of your father's,"
said Mrs. Chapman.

So we went to the prom after all
where Paula danced with everyone else.
As I stood by the wall drinking quantities
of pink lemonade out of paper cups
her laughter rang like a chime of bells.

*

I didn't see her for years
while I was in the army.

42

Then we made up for lost time
at the movies, in the balcony . . .
on my sofa that converted into a bed . . .
and under the trees — it was summer —
at night on Riverside Drive.

"Spry for Baking" said the sign
shining above the Palisades.
A barge with its warning lights
would be going up the Hudson . . .
the George Washington Bridge
gleaming in the moonlight
against the scudding clouds.

"That's it," said Paula. "There."

*

"Are you all right?" says Eubie.
I nod. I'm not going to let on.
Though I brush after every meal,
when she gives me the paper cup
with the liquid that's bright red
and bitter . . . and I have held it in my mouth
for thirty seconds, spat it out,
and rinsed with the mouthwash,
and she hands me the mirror,
there are always some traces
of the plaque that causes decay.

*

Mrs. Chapman didn't approve of me.
It took me some time to catch on.
"He's too," she told Paula, "bohemian."

She was saving her precious daughter
for someone able to provide her

with the better things of life:
wall-to-wall carpeting and dark brown furniture.

Paula wanted to "be in the theater."
So her mother packed her off
to some second-rate school in Boston
where they taught it . . . whatever it was.

Actors, I told her, weren't people.
Like monkeys or parrots
they could repeat sounds and simulate feelings
but had none of their own.

"Don't call me," she said, "I'll call you."

               *

She was as good as her word . . .
she called, twenty years later.
She had just "winged in" from the Coast
and was staying at a friend's apartment
in Soho. There was a restaurant
right on the corner.

I recognized her at once
though she was wearing a pants suit
and big glasses with rhinestones
and the skin that used to look like
some marvellous tropical fruit
was sallow . . . and the glossy black hair
was still black, but lusterless like ink.

The expressions that used to be endearing . . .
fluttering her eyelashes,
touching her tongue to her top lip,
were like the moving eyelids and mouth
of a doll.

And the shop talk!
She kept dropping names
of people in Hollywood and Beverly Hills
I'd never heard of or wanted to.

I said as much. I could hear myself
sneering, like Diogenes in a washtub.
And what did I have to feel so
superior about?
Where were my screen credits? Did I own a swimming pool?

More to the point . . .
where was the novel I was going to write
that would put Proust in the shade?

                              *

The magic, as they say, was gone,
like a song that used to be on the hit parade.

But there is always a new song,
and some things never change.
Not long ago, visiting a friend
who lives on Riverside Drive
I saw that the sign for Spry
is still there, shining away.

"Spry for Baking." It blinks off
and on again . . . "For Frying."
Then the lights run around in a circle.

ED

Ed was in love with a cocktail waitress,
but Ed's family, and his friends,
didn't approve. So he broke it off.

He married a respectable woman
who played the piano. She played well enough
to have been a professional.

Ed's wife left him . . .
Years later, at a family gathering

Ed got drunk and made a fool of himself.
He said, "I should have married Doreen."
"Well," they said, "why didn't you?"

BERNIE

Bernie was part Lithuanian
and part American Indian.
He weighed over two hundred pounds.
My earliest memory of Bernie
has to do with his weight. The university
assigned Bernie, who was some sort of
administrative assistant,
to help me and my wife find a house.

We found a big one — three stories
and a wide porch. Bernie stood on the porch
and jumped, and jumped again,
coming down hard with his cowboy boots.
The floor thundered, but it held.
"That's how you test a house," Bernie said.

We became friends
travelling together to a writers' conference
in Montreal . . . and collapsed,
rolling with laughter, streaming tears,
when the poet from Bengal read his masterpiece,
"Tiki, tiki, parakeety."

We flew to Washington, and marched
in a protest against the war.
Bernie, who was deathly afraid of flying,
got drunk in the airport.
He was also afraid of getting his head busted,
and shook all the way. The peace march
was uneventful where we were.
I walked beside a Benedictine monk
from Minnesota. In other parts of the march
the right things were happening to famous men.

That night Bernie left the hotel
to find a woman.

He came back at two in the morning
completely broke and filled with contrition:
"Why do I do these things to myself?"
He sat on the bed making long-distance calls.
Then he said, "Do you have any money?"
I lent him fifteen dollars and he went out again.

He wanted to write, that was why
he was at the university. But he despised
the chickenshit department of English.
He also despised the literary life
in New York, all the *apparatchiki*
named Howard or Norman.

So it came as no surprise
when one day he just suddenly
up and left, with his hound Sylvia
and wife June, whom I've forgotten to mention —
an intelligent, beautiful woman
from a family in Butte that almost died
when she married this part Lithuanian,
part Oglala Sioux,
part pork barrel and part bear.

From time to time one of his books would appear.
Then, as can only happen in America,
he was famous. I heard he was being offered
thirty-thousand-dollar advances.
He went to Hollywood and made a movie.
I saw it . . . it was set in North Dakota.
Two men go hunting in the woods
and have some wild adventures.

When I came home from the movie
I didn't go in, but stood on the porch for a while.
The stars were shining above the trees
and roofs and telephone poles.
Upstairs Alma and the kids were asleep,

safe and snug. I could still see where
Bernie's cowboy heels had hit the floor.
There were half-moon indentations.
The wood was, as they say, distressed.

And so am I. The people I care about
live in different parts of the country
and we no longer keep in touch.

ELEGY FOR JAKE

Taking off the old paint
layer by layer . . .
"Let Zip-Strip do the work."

It is also necessary to scrape.
No one driving by the house
on a quiet Saturday
would know that in the cellar
machine guns, bangalore torpedoes
and eighty-eight-millimeter shells
were going off.

                Or that the shadows
of women were complaining,
"You don't care for anyone but yourself."

Stamping out with a suitcase in one hand,
the reading lamp in the other . . .

Fumes. Open a window
and prop it, the cord being gone,
with *Great Love Stories*, edited by Jake Harmon.

Big Jake, who would be called on to speak
at every important publishers' gathering,
whose sayings were always being quoted
in the *Saturday Review* and the *Times* . . .

Stabbed in the back by his partner.
There was blood on a green, felt-covered table.
He lingered a few years, dying slowly,
moving from place to place.
At the end of a long corridor
the room in which he sat was piled with books.
A window looked across the air shaft

to a ledge where pigeons built their nests.
Here the traffic was hushed,
so that you heard the *rou* and *rou*
of the pigeons. They fluttered,
ruffled, and pecked.
The shadows of their wings
flashed across a sunlit wall.

He had been put in charge of a "cultural series" —
books with a limited audience
but "viable cultural interest."

Why weep for Jake?
Those who live by expense accounts
perish by them. On Madison Avenue
I see in people's faces
marks of some internal bleeding,
fears of slipping, losing one's job.
With one boy at Yale, the other at Deerfield . . .

But before this comes to pass
it is summer. Leafy boughs
of oak and elm are rustling.
Jake is in jeans, with the overnight guest
helping build a split-rail fence.
Jake always makes his weekend guests
help with the chores. It gives them a taste
of living in the country.

He is at the moment of his greatest happiness.
He has just been named Editor of the Year.

Later, on the patio, over frankfurters
and beer — lemonade for the children —
he is talking about Flaubert
to Dick Weinstein, who listens deferentially.
Jake is the intellectual, Dick
the partner who manages finances

at Hyperion Books. Jake and Dick
and their wives are a foursome,
going to restaurants and shows together,
and the wives always on the telephone.

Flaubert, Jake is saying,
was a sadist. Keeping his boots on
while making love to a woman!
He will never forgive him for this.
Besides, Flaubert had no imagination —
you can see it in *Sentimental Education*.

He praises his most recent discovery.
A friend of Adlai Stevenson
has written a novel . . .
"the best thing of its kind
since *War and Peace*. I mean it sincerely."

And he did. That was the secret
of Jake's success. His sincerity.

So one day he went into the boardroom.
Weinstein and the other two partners
were there. And copies of Jake's books —
all the books he'd contracted to publish —
were piled on the table.

                    "Mandy,"
Dick said, turning to his secretary,
"you can start." And she began reading
sales figures.

Do you recall *King Richard the Third*
where he keeps the council waiting,
and Hastings is getting nervous
and talks compulsively of Richard,
what a good friend he has been,
and how you can always tell Richard's feelings

by what you see in his face . . .
And the other men seated at the table
start drawing away from Hastings
until they're all at the far end
and he's sitting alone?

So Jake sat, while the figures
went rolling off like doom.
Finally it was finished. "Jake,"
Dick Weinstein said, "you're out."

As I said, he lingered for some years.
The last time I saw him, on Martha's Vineyard,
he had grown a beard . . .
I suppose, to go with the cultural series.

Playing it back. Scraping paint . . .
Shadows flutter and fly across a wall.

AKHMATOVA'S HUSBAND

Akhmatova's husband, Gumilev,
was a poet and an explorer.
He wrote poems about wild animals
and had fantastic ideas:
a red bird with the head of a girl
and a lost tram that goes wandering . . .

shedding fire "like a storm with dark wings,"
passing over bridges,
by a house with three windows
where a woman he loved once lived,
and, rushing toward him,
two raised hooves and an iron glove.

Gumilev fought in the Great War
with almost incredible valor,
twice winning the Cross of Saint George.
He envisioned a little old man
forging the bullet that would kill him.

It wasn't a German bullet, it was Russian.
Gumilev was killed by his own countrymen
as poets in Russia frequently are.

Everyone talks about Akhmatova
but no one talks about Gumilev.
That wouldn't have mattered to Gumilev.
When the man from the government came to kill him,
"Just give me a cigarette," said Gumilev,
"and let's get it over with."

IV
RED-AVOIDING
PICTURES

RED-AVOIDING PICTURES

In Japan many years ago
when tides of hate surging to and fro
left heads impaled on fences
and the rivers stained with blood,

painters would work in other colors,
brown, yellow, green and blue . . .
beni-girai-e. I too
prefer to make a "red-avoiding picture."

THE CHAMPION SINGLE SCULLS

Green leaves lit by the sun,
the rest deep in shadow . . .
a tree is an adequate symbol
of inner or spiritual life.
("The natural object," said E. P.,
"is always the adequate symbol.")

It wasn't just characters . . .
one heard that successful men,
corporation executives, were into
transcendental meditation.
But now they have given it up,
they are into tennis and running.

Though I have prayed with Eliot,
"Teach us to sit still,"
this could be laziness,
and life could be very dull.
Besides, the wicked are not still,
they are sharpening a sword.

*

Stillness, said a picture,
is not being immobile,
but a clear separation
of the self from its surroundings
while taking part (we must take part,
how else are we to live?)

"Max Schmitt in a Single Scull" . . .
A river with iron bridges . . .
Schmitt is resting on his oars,
looking toward the observer,
"both in and out of the game."
Rowing! This is what I have to practice.

A FINE DAY FOR STRAW HATS

He bought an old ship's lifeboat,
gave it an engine,
and built on a roof extending
from the stern to the bow.
It looked like a house, but it ran.

He christened it *Seahawk*,
and we travelled across the harbor
to Port Royal . . . sand and coconuts,
a few houses and huts,
and a low wall with embrasures
for cannon. This was Fort Charles
where Nelson used to stand
gazing at the sun and the pelicans.

And there were streets and ruins
in the weedy ooze below . . .
the pirate town that vanished
in an earthquake long ago.

*

The trip back was monotonous,
the fan of the wake subsiding
in foam, the thrumming of the engine . . .

When a ship had anchored in the harbor
we would go slowly around it
and read the name on the stern.

There used to be white steamers,
the Grace Line, sailing the Caribbean.
We saw the *Empress of Britain*,

and once, the battle cruiser *Rodney*.
I imagined the big guns firing,

the flame and smoke of battle,
ships sliding beneath the waves.

*

One Christmas we were in the *Seahawk*
off Kingston. An excursion launch
was setting out, crowded with passengers,
straw hats and gaily colored frocks.

I gazed away, to the Palisades . . .
behind them a sleeve of smoke
unravelling . . . a ship at sea.

When I looked again the excursion launch
had vanished. There were only seagulls,
and a confused murmur
coming from the people on shore.

We steered where the launch had been
and circled. The garden boy,
who also served as an able seaman,
fished up something with the boat hook . . .
a man's straw hat.
He placed it on the seat and we stared at it.

Next day's *Gleaner* carried the story:
the launch had capsized,
more than forty were feared drowned.

I don't think I was frightened
so much as appalled. That this could happen
at Christmas, on a calm sea . . .

Nothing, the sea whispers, is certain.

*

Reflections of the harbor
flit on walls. On the veranda
leaves are rustling. In the afternoon
a breeze springs up, driving whitecaps
into shore. The tops of the palms
thrash and swerve.

Sea clouds are drifting over.
Years, and a house seems to drift
and hills appear to have moved.

But memory is secure,
it is anchored with a chain.
Nothing short of a hurricane
could ever tear it loose.

A REMEMBRANCE OF THINGS PAST

For a long time I stayed in bed
reading Proust, in the two Random House volumes
wherever they happened to fall open.

For the truth is not in chronology,
day turning to dusk in the street outside.
Real time is inside one's head . . .
the white hawthorn blossoms at Combray.
Balbec by the foam-lined sea.

The doctor, a friend of Cottard's,
diagnosed my condition as "neurasthenic."

And if you aren't rich, and don't have servants . . .
So I got out of bed finally,
and carried Proust kicking down the hall
to the incinerator, and dropped him in.

A heavy thud. A second . . .

*

The man who stopped me on the bank of the Seine
to tell his story, was a Frenchman
of middle age. He had obviously had a few.

"You are," he said, "American,
and would never have heard of Proust.
Monsieur Proust was a writer, a great man.
I was his companion and chauffeur.

One day when I entered the apartment
I put a hand on the wall.
For days and months afterwards

Monsieur Proust would go over to the wall
to see if there was still a mark."

He delivered this as proof.
There, you see,
that is what it is to have genius!

*

He is wearing a cloth cap, the sign
of the European "man of forty."
He has a moustache, a pink complexion
heightened with wine.

He invites me to come and visit him —
he owns a hotel — and talk about Proust.

I can see the published interview,
maybe even a *New Yorker* "profile."

But what would this have to do
with Proust . . . a rushing of traffic
through the streets of Manhattan at dusk,
windows suddenly lighting up,
the radio in the next apartment,
murmur of voices and clatter of dishes?

I thanked him, and did not go.

THE GARDENER

She is on her knees pulling weeds.
Her soul is desirous, it longs for cucumbers
and melons if they will grow.

When the earth was without form, and void,
and darkness upon the face of the deep,
the soul was born, a piece of the void

broken off . . . the winged Psyche,
Desire, who is always wandering
over these lawns and between these houses.

She clings for a while
to a flower or a book, then launches
once more her little sail.

REFLECTIONS IN A SPA

The walls are lined with mirrors,
doubling their images, front and back.
You see yourself receding in a tunnel.

The man on the adjacent bicycle
speaks: "Whakunam?"
Finally I understand: he has no voice box.
"Whakunam?" means "What's your name?"
"Amjaw" — "I am George."

There are impressive physical specimens:
body builders, weight lifters
with limbs of oak, bellies ridged like washboards.
On the other hand, some whose doctors
have said, "Exercise, or else!"

And some like George, and a night watchman
whose legs are withered and walks
dragging each foot across the floor,
like a "partially destroyed insect" —
the cripple Doyle in *Miss Lonelyhearts*.

The time will pass more easily
thinking about *Miss Lonelyhearts*.
Without fiction life would be hell.

I feel like a disembodied spirit.
Who is that balding middle-aged man
in the mirror, pedalling away from me?
Strange, the back of one's own head
and body growing small.

IN OTTO'S BASEMENT

At the meeting of the village board
last night in Otto's basement
when they were discussing a building violation —
Why hasn't the building inspector reported?
The village lawyer is waiting to hear from him.
The inspector has to be told to "get off the pot" —
a picture drifted into my mind
from some Latin American country,
of men tied to posts, about to be shot.
Or perhaps it was Africa, or Afghanistan.

So we endure it. This is what Jefferson
and Lincoln had to endure,
sitting and listening to people
argue . . . the cost of conversion from oil to coal
and the statement by the tree-trimming committee.
If you want to know what freedom cost
look for us here, under the linoleum.
Dig between the end of the table
and the wall of some brown material
grained like wood, with imitation knotholes.

IN A TIME OF PEACE

He changes dollars into francs
and walks, from Rue de Rivoli
almost to the Arc de Triomphe.

He sits at a sidewalk café
and looks at the ones who are passing.
Then goes to a restaurant
and a show.

        Someone told him the Crazy Horse
is the place to go, "un spectacle de deux heures"
you can understand "if you're Javanese,
dead drunk, or mentally retarded."
There are sketches, stripteases:
blonde Solange, black Marianne,
Ingrid with her boots and whip . . .
and who can forget Duzia,
"the most wanted girl in Europe"?

The chorus in the entractes
jump and squeal. Imagining
their own nudity is driving them mad.

After the show he chooses to walk.
The lamps in leafy avenues
shining on monuments and statues . . .

*

A sea of amethyst is breaking
along two miles of beach umbrellas . . .
the car parks, red roofs
of the bathing establishments,
Lidino, Antaura . . . advertisements
for Stock, Coca-Cola,
"tutte le Sera DISCOTECA."

A child on the crowded sand
is playing with a new toy.
It hurls an object into the air,
a parachute opens, it descends . . .
homunculus, a little plastic man
returning from Outer Space.

Some day we may have to live there,
but for the present life consists
of sex . . . all the beautiful bodies
that you see on the beach;
food — there are dozens of places,
ranging from the ice-cream parlor
to Tito's — Ristorante Tito del Molo;
things to buy: Galletti for handbags,
Timpano for a lighter;
and entertainment: the Cinema Odeon,
the bar with pinball machines.
There is even a Sauna Finlandese.

At night the promenade glitters,
loud music fills the air.
Not good music . . . but it doesn't matter
to the families with small children
or to the lovers.